## *Introduction to dreamers*

We all have dreams within the depths of our heart that we aspire to achieve. We all have a dream life, and a lifestyle that we aspire to live. Often, we do not pursue those dreams let alone fulfill our life's purpose. If you once had a dream that you let die this book is for you. If you are one who is currently pursuing your dreams and you need that extra boost of encouragement, don't worry you chose the right book. If your dream has been chewed up spit out and stepped on you need this book. You will receive that encouragement that you need to move forward towards the dream that you love so dearly. I will teach you a unique way of looking at your dream. I will also give you practical steps on how to achieve your dream as fast as possible.

One of the biggest reasons why people don't achieve their dreams is because there are obstacles standing in the way of that. One of the biggest obstacles is the question most Christians fall captive to which is: Is my dream in the will of God for my life? In the book I go into detail about how your dream fits in the plan of God. I also clarify misconceptions of whether you are to act or just let God do it. As you pursue your dream you must understand that there are dream snatchers all around you but the biggest way that your dream can be stolen from you is through fear and distraction.

I'm going to give you various

characters you know from the Holy Scripture who struggled with fear and distractions. I will also give you details about my life and how God brought me through the process of overcoming fear and distractions. If your dream comes from a sincere place, you must know that your dream is tied to your purpose somehow. I like to think of it as your dream being the daughter of your purpose. In other words, your purpose in life is the bigger picture. If you can't start fulfilling your dreams in life, how will you fulfill your purpose? If I was your enemy and I did not want, you to fulfill your purpose and dreams I would simply try to distract you or make you fearful. By the end of this book, you should have a clear view of your vision so that nothing can hinder you this time around.

    Sit back, get a cup of tea, put your feet up and relax. You're about to receive some answers that you've been waiting for. Get ready to cast aside all those heavy expectations that you have allowed to keep you from fulfilling your dream. As I was authoring this book, I was very prayerful and thankful for God giving me the words for everyone who would read it and be moved to action. If you picked this book up it means that this title is connected to a part of you that wants to fulfill your dream, a part of you that desires to see beauty in your life. If you are one who has nothing more than a dream, you want to start pursuing it now but don't know the first step, this book will be a blessing to you as it inspires and motivates you to run toward your dream. If you have already begun fulfilling your dream but for whatever reason there's a loss of enthusiasm and motivation and now you can't find a good enough reason to pick up and push through, this book is for you. It will teach you how to have a conquerors mentality so that you can bring your dream to pass faster than you ever thought possible. Enjoy!

Heaven Brown

## Content Table

**Chapter 1- Pursuing your dream.**

**Chapter 2- What is my purpose.**

**Chapter 3- How to execute my dream.**

**Chapter 4- Dream connection**

**Chapter 5- The biggest hindrance is Fear.**

**Chapter 6- Fear of rejection**

**Chapter 7- Fear of failure**

**Chapter 8- Your dream will declare war.**

**Chapter 9-While on your dream cloud**

Heaven Brown

*Your Dream Your Responsibility*

# Chapter 1
# Pursuing your dream?

**Create your own world.**
There's blessedness in the hands of humanity, and a gift that allows us to create our own world. Somehow, we humans have the capacity to take a portion of a rugged, nasty swamp and create a beautiful, refreshing, lovely park, all because we can use our imagination and dream beyond what our eyes can see.

Picture the earth and all the beauty that we experience daily, some parts are natural beauties because of God's imagination. Other parts of the world are shaped and landscaped from the imagination and creativity of humans.

## Your Dream Your Responsibility

We have been given the ability to change what once was an ugly looking world after the fall, to a beautiful and comfortable home for human beings. Yes! We live in a fallen world, but it doesn't mean our imagination and dreams has to be to be fallen. I'm telling you today; if you can dream beyond your eyes, you have it within your power to create anything that you desire. You are already gifted with the ability to shape and create your own world.

Early 2015, I started to become inspired about creating my world. I realized I have the creativity within myself to create my own world. People are given opportunities because of the creative gifts they have. I never really knew how creative I was and how it could benefit me. Before a gift is discovered, it must first be uncovered; before a gift can be uncovered, it must start with a pursuit; before it can be pursued, one must challenge themselves to birth it out of their imagination. Some of us never pay attention to the good things that come from our imagination.

Because God wanted you here, He took His imagination and spoke it into existence. Awesome right! Just like God, we can imagine our dreams and create our world. I see people who create all types of businesses, which would have never been thought of without a creative imagination; however, through the gift of imagination we have the capacity to create our world. We can even create our world with our own words. Whether you are aware of it or not, your imagination feeds your dream the food that it needs to stay creative. If you don't use your imagination, you can't have a dream.

Earlier in 2014, I put a sticker above my bed that said, "Dream until your dreams come true." I placed the sticker there to remind myself that no matter where I fall in this place called life, I never want to lose sight of the original dreams that were placed in my heart. Some of us are unaware that our dreams are connected to our soul; when your dream is stolen it is a sign that your soul is not fulfilled. Our dreams uniquely sprout from the soul (mind, will, and emotions) of the person who imagined them. If you have a grand idea of being someone great, do not allow anyone to influence you so much that they discourage your imagination and steal your dreams entirely. For this reason, some have a vexed soul, they know they're supposed to pursue greatness, but a stolen dream creates an empty and unfulfilled Life.

# Your Dream Your Responsibility

### Pursuing that dream

I believe there must be a balance between seeking signs of the right time and positioning yourself for your dream life. How awesome is it, when you experience confirmation on everything that you have set your heart out to do, receiving direction on your path every step of the way? Everything is falling in line, and you can tell, this is your time.

When you have an overwhelming desire to start your dream, it's usually because there's a seed sewn in your heart. If you have ideas, inventions or businesses, then they are your responsibility. You cannot be timid about your Dream. People who are timid usually have a mentality that says, "If it's meant to be for me, it will happen." In my opinion, this is a peasant mentality. The only way peasants receive is when someone else gives to them. Keep in mind; if you never pursue it, it will never happen.

I've noticed that I've gotten ideas

in the past; instead of doing the legwork, I thought of every excuse as to why I shouldn't pursue it. If you have an idea, you cannot be afraid to pursue it. After all there is an appointed time for the fulfillment of every dream. You've been given the idea today instead of yesterday because today is the appointed time for you to start pursuing it. Figure out the steps you need to take to get there and when you feel the time is right go after it.

In 2013, I started getting speaking engagements; people were contacting me unexpectedly. I was ready to go forward, but I was not good at staying connected with people or asking them for opportunities, because I assumed it would just happen for me. This procrastinating mindset kept me enslaved to believing that I was too gifted to lift a finger.

We have it on the inside of us to make our lives whatever we want. No one is stopping us, if it isn't happening it's only because we are getting in our own way. My friend and I went to a festival once; after we paid our way at the door, we began to walk down the aisle of the festival. It had vendor shops and food stands on both sides, but the aisle was short-lived and only stretched for about one fourth of a mile. It was very disappointing because we were under the impression that it was a huge festival. We thought we would meet more vendors, authors, business owners, and even have more food options. We got to the end and there was a guy who had a T-shirt stand, he was waiting for us to come to his stand, but he saw that we were not interested so he decided to get up and come to us. He spoke negative words about the festival. He said, "Do you see how much these people think of us? They couldn't even give us more options for the festival." He suggested that we should be offended because the festival was a real rip-off. I walked away because his approach was extremely negative. I realized that this man is the only person in his own way; he developed a concept for why he was oppressed.

At some point we must take responsibility for our own lives. We all have an equal opportunity to make our dream a reality. All of us have it within our power to make our own lives beautiful; in America we all have freedom and liberty to make our dreams come to the past. His oppression was deeply rooted in his mentality and his views on life. I am aware that there are barriers that are put in place to keep the oppressed more oppressed, but I am convinced that I'm in control of the outcome of my life and my purpose. Keep in mind there are many influences, but you are the executive decision maker in your world! Be encouraged and know that your life changes when you change your mindset.

***I would rather use others.*** 

The way we view money as an opportunity to come up is the same way we often view other people as an opportunity to come up. People who view others to increase usually treat everyone who comes into their life as nothing more than money to be spent.

Their mindset is 'how can I use this person to the best of my ability?' If you're a part of their life, they can eventually suck you dry. Often when you do offer to help, they will usually end up begging for more as if you are obligated. God, forbid you don't help them out; the next trick they try is the guilt trip. These are the kind of people that cast their responsibilities on other people rather than take responsibility for their own lives. They always blame others for why they are unable to do things for themselves. This is someone who'd rather other people bring their dream to them on a silver platter. If we genuinely want to see our dream meet our future, we cannot be one of those people who depend on or use others instead of going to get it ourselves. If someone isn't helping you with your dream, please don't take it personal, just know that your dream is your responsibility!

If this has been your mentality, I want to release you from the ignorance of believing that you can be lazy, and your dreams will still happen to you.

For some people it happens immediately because they just so happen to be in the right place at the right time, but for others it's not so easy. If you want to eat, you must go after your meal. I noticed that God gives us resources, but He will not cheat for us. The resources are to equip you to pursue and obtain, but if you never get out of bed to go do the legwork, you will never increase. Please! Whatever you do, don't allow yourself to think with a lazy mentality. People will not do the work for you, they can help you along the way as you seek counsel, but it is up to you to execute your dream on your own. "It always seems impossible until it's done", Nelson Mandela.

**Use your imagination.**

I encourage everyone to think outside of the box and get creative with their imagination and thoughts. The thing about creative imagination is that you cannot go wrong. Something may be a bit far-fetched from your budget, but all things are possible. Now we know that even the moon is reachable because humanity used his imagination to get there. Be fearful for what? Sir Winston Churchill said, "Success is the ability to go from failure to failure, without a loss of enthusiasm." If you are one who has failed a few times to the point that people have laughed at you, I'm telling you to rejoice and be happy because you, my friend, are on the path of success! Do not let the fear of failure and what others think ruin your imagination or your dream.

**An unworthy dreamer**

It's so heartbreaking when I see people who are afraid to go forward. In some cases, it's because of the unknown. In other cases, it's a lack of confidence. Unbelievably, there are a lot of people who struggle with self-worth, which is why getting started on their dream seems so far away to them. Before you step into your dream, you must know that you are already worth your dream. Yes, you can have it and yes, you're worth it. We are usually too concerned with what everyone else thinks. Self-worth issues are usually rooted from some sort of mental abuse received by others in the past. The weird thing about self-worth is that it is a borrowed, inaccurate depiction of you. If you have borrowed someone else's opinion or views of yourself, you must give it back before stepping foot toward your dream. You will need to reconsider the lies that you believed in the past about you and your inability.

Understand that impossibilities turn into abilities, when we decide to step outside of ourselves, understand our true value, and shoot for our highest dream. This feeling of unworthiness is one of the main reasons people don't succeed. They can be successful in many endeavors yet reach a point and don't feel like they deserve it. Don't let anyone tell you that you don't deserve to reap the benefits of your own blessings, especially when you have worked hard for every ounce of what comes to you. Remember you are 100 percent worthy.

## Your Dream Your Responsibility

Some of us don't want to make moves because we're afraid that people will think we are trying to be too important. If you pursue a dream, understand that people are going to think whatever they want, but it has nothing to do with you or the dream inside of you. It's true that some people have self-worth issues, and they go to the extreme and become over flashy and unrealistic in their image. They start to buy expensive things to show off. Everything they do is to prove to others their self-worth because they don't know it. Then you have some who do the opposite. These individuals know their self-worth and genuinely desire to express it, but because of the fear of what other people will say they take the lowly road and become frustrated in their contentment. They have the tendency to have an attitude that says, 'Woe is me.' People who find themselves in these circumstances are so focused on what others think of them, that they never fulfill their own purpose. No matter what, along our journey we cannot be fueled by the opinions of others, because keeping up a façade is not realistic, and neither is being a victim to unworthiness.

# Chapter 2

# What is my Purpose?

**Self-Awareness**

Before you start each day, you should genuinely dedicate yourself to being self-aware and keeping a sense of peace within. Pursuing that peace every morning will ignite a more centered confident peace within yourself and others you meet. Keeping in mind that you have a purpose and knowing that your life is worth something bigger that people can see will motivate you to stay joyful and happy. When life starts to get us down, we naturally revert to thoughts of our purpose and begin asking ourselves why we're here in the first place. When people can't see anything good in their view, they start thinking of suicide and a way to end the agony of being purposeless. This is why keeping a centered sense of self-awareness and knowing that God made us with a purpose can led to a more positive outlook on life.

Your purpose and your call are intertwined, and there is no way that you can understand every aspect of it through just a simple conversation or reading a book. I am convinced that our purpose is in the bigger picture and that our purpose is always unfolding as we go on in life. We usually come to discover that various things had to happen to get us to where we are right now. Sometimes life can seem so purposeless, especially when you have nothing to look forward to, or you feel you've fallen off from your original plan. But again, our purpose is the bigger picture and if you can remember that your purpose is being revealed every day; feeling purposeless is a part of life. I believe, we all need to pay attention to that internal alarm that serves as a reminder that "all things are working together for our good because we love God and are called according to Gods purpose." Romans 8:28

I believe everyone deserves to breathe easy and to experience the beauty of living a wonderful life. How many of us take the time to imagine our lives being complete and whole? I believe our lives will begin to fill up with wholeness when we start to fulfill our dreams. Every time you achieve a dream you allow more victory to enter your life giving you the fuel you need to keep going. I have news for you, there is a victory that we are all called to walk in, it is the fulfillment of our purpose that was predestined for us. Each day that our purpose begins to unfold, 'living the good life' becomes more achievable. You start to feel yourself getting closer and closer to where you know you're supposed to be.

**Calculated Days**

After the flood on Noah's day, our

lifespan was reduced significantly. If you go by the Gregorian international calendar, also known as the 'Western calendar' consisting of dates based on time. This calendar was adopted and introduced in February 1582 by Pope Gregory XIII. I will be using this calendar as an analogy to help us calculate our days.

In the biblical days, our lifespan was between 800-900 years, after the flood God reduced them significantly to around 120 years. When you do the calculations and divide those years into days, it is interesting to know that those who lived 900 years lived for around 300,000 days in total. Those who lived 120 years, lived approximately 40,000 days. But now, the average life expectancy of a Human is 90 years maximum, and the lifespan of a 90-year-old is only approximately 30,000 days.

Let's just say you sat down and wanted to plan out exactly how those days may be spent. The first 10,000 would consist of growing up and getting an education. Another 8000 would be dedicated to raising children and trying to figure out what your purpose is. 5000 spent working and maintaining business. 5000 spent pursuing your dreams. 2000 spent fulfilling the call on your life. Though some of these years overlap and this breakdown looks different for different people, this is a hypothetical analogy for the purpose of getting you to understand that we can decide exactly how these days should be spent. Please understand that you do not have very much time and every day is important.

### Purpose Starts with a Dream

When I began to understand that my days were numbered, I realized that I am here for distinct reasons. I understand that my purpose is a daily walk-through life. Your purpose is bigger than one specific thing. Your purpose can consist of childbearing, being a doctor, being a motivational speaker or becoming a lawyer. You are purposed for all these things, and you are not limited to just one of them. You were created to hold many titles such as Author, CEO, Doctor, Judge, Father, Sister, and so on and so forth. In other words, your purpose can literally the fulfillment of your desires and dreams. Your purpose will ultimately uncover a message about your love, your character and the way you live your life. Sometimes the purpose of an individual can seem so unclear until they have passed away; This is when the world suddenly understands why you walked the path you did while here on earth. Even if you don't understand your complete purpose, I challenge you to go along with Gods leading and do whatever He is calling you to do. All the pieces of the puzzle will eventually align and after each victory you will understand more about your purpose.

Remember, your dream can be viewed as the daughter of your purpose, we know that a mother can have as many children as she wishes to complete her family. Your purpose will start to feel achieved when you are on the path to fulfilling your dreams. As your purpose unfolds daily, you will start to see that you were not placed here on this earth just to do one thing.

I've had people ask me about their calling and how they should pursue it. There are some misconceptions about our purpose versus our call. The calling is a broad statement as well as your life's purpose. The calling has many different sides attached to it. When I turned 20, I started getting revelations about the call that was on my life. I assumed this call to the ministry was my purpose. What I did not understand was that it was not my complete purpose, but merely a part of it. I now know that my purpose is to do the will of God, have a family, speak into the lives of others, help as many people as possible and fulfill my dreams big and small. Furthermore, I know that this is just a part of my purpose in life.

Remember, your call is not your purpose, and your purpose is not your call. If you have a call in your life, do not limit yourself to just that call. If you have a dream that you have envisioned for years, do not limit yourself to just that dream. We should continue to have an open mind when it comes to our future. I was so happy when I got this revelation, because for a while, I was trained to believe that I was only destined to become just one thing in life.

Back in school, whenever a new class would start, the teacher would ask the students to introduce themselves and to tell the class what they would like to be when they grow up. Many of the students would shout out answers that they thought were cool and some would be more specific by saying a lawyer, doctor, pilot, nurse or teacher. All these answers were great but notice that we were only encouraged to say one thing that we wanted to be. I took it differently than the way the question was intended. Unbelievably, as simple and innocent as the question appears to a child, it is the very question that shapes the way they see their lives. I went through life assuming that I could only be one thing.

The teacher was not asking the question to limit me, but rather to get me to open my mind to the possibility of greatness. Even though I forgot half of the answers that I gave, somehow, I still believed that I was only destined to be one thing in life. Growing up, I searched for my purpose. I understand the concept of having a degree consisting of a couple of different concentrations, but because society believes that if you master one thing well, you will get the largest amount of return on your investment.

Although I believe there are some truths to this concept, I also believe that it can be accidentally interpreted in the wrong way, a way that limits people. The truth is a person is more respected when they can say they've been a nurse for 18 years. But it is even more exciting to see this person walking into their purpose that they were supposed to fulfil, especially when they see no need to stop there. Instead of being content at a job that you are not happy with calling your purpose, I suggest you take the limits off yourself by thinking you are only purposed for one thing. Dream big, and when you begin to fulfill your purpose, you give others the opportunity to enjoy you at your best.

The reason this is so important is because I see so many people in jobs and careers that they really hate. They are unfulfilled and discouraged, after spending four years getting a degree that they come to realize they never really wanted to begin with. They also have the added pressure of paying off their student loans. The main reason people choose the careers that they have is usually due to the financial benefits that will significantly cover their household expenses. Most people would rather stay home and earn a living from their business, than punch the clock for the career that they cannot stand.

It's so sad to see people in this situation, people who want so much more out of life, but instead, they settle and eventually forget about the dream that they once had. Maybe it requires too much time, money and energy to start something new. I want to encourage you that it is never too late for you to fulfill your dream. You are not dead, so there is no reason you cannot get started. Forget about the impossibilities that will come to discourage you and make you feel as though it can never happen. We must have faith that the impossible is possible. The older you get, the more odds you will have against you, which means you will have more obstacles to overcome. This is why you cannot wait another day! Your dream belongs to you! It is your responsibility to get up and redeem it! If there are any resources that you need, there be no more delay! Go for it.

# Heaven Brown

# Chapter 3
# How to execute my dream

Let's Get Practical

Your dreams should be important to you individually because your dream is something that you had the ability to birth on your own. If you are one who has a dream but don't understand how to really execute that dream, I want to share a few things with you that will help you make your dream a reality soon. One of the first things we must keep in mind is that our dreams are only as real as we make them, there is no way we can expect someone else to come along and make our dream a reality first. You must be the one to step up and say to yourself 'my dream is worth me pursuing on my own'. The truth is that no one else is going to care about your dream if you don't care about your dream yourself. I'm going to give you nine things that you must have so that you can make your dream a reality. Some of them might not pertain to your dream, but you will find that these principals are important for everyone with a dream especially if you are starting your own business:

1. Cast your vision

2. Enthusiasm and confidence

3. Research and planning

4. Schooling and training

5. Formatting and presentation

6. Marketing and networking

7. Consistency and discipline

8. Staying focused

9. Setting a deadline

These steps do depend very much on what your dream calls for, but my goal is to cover the entire basis.

## 1. Cast Your Vision

To have a vision of your dream is like having a finished product or an imaginary prototype. Your vision helps you to stay focused while formatting and bringing it to fruition. Bringing it all together in your mind and putting it on paper gives you a detailed view of the full picture, you must write it down and create what you want the ending to look like.

You might ask why it needs to be on tablets or paper. My answer to that is, when you write it out, it becomes established. For some reason as humans, we are more prone to feel the need to complete something if it is written down rather than spoken or kept in our mind. Furthermore, it helps those around you to get a clear view of how to execute this task. Some people depending on their dream see fit to go a step further and write down their mission which is what informs people of why they do what they do. If you have a dream, I encourage you to write an action plan and cast your vision as soon as possible.

## 2. Enthusiasm and Confidence

Enthusiasm is especially important when it comes to pursuing your dream. Your enthusiasm is the life and the fuel to your dream. If your enthusiasm is low, the chances are your dream will not happen as fast as you would like. You cannot be casual when you are pursuing your dream, the more aggressive you are the better. It's like a person who is so hungry that they know they will die if they don't eat. Your dream is your meal, it's your life and how you choose to survive. If you don't have the gas to do the legwork, there is no way you will see it come to pass like you desire.

When I say enthusiasm, I'm referring to your excitement and your passion about your dream. If you're not on fire to achieve it, no one else will do it for you. Throughout the entire process of pursuit, you must stay enthusiastic. A few things that can help you stay enthusiastic are doing constant research, planning, setting dates to make minor purchases and getting other enthusiastic people excited about your dream. Your dream should be such a reality that you see it in its complete imaginary form before it happens.

I once had a similar conversation with a lady who really wanted to pursue her dream, but every time she starts to build momentum for it, she looks at someone else's achievement and at once becomes discouraged. This was her excuse for not pursuing her dream. I felt sad for her because it meant that her dreams were contingent upon her emotions at the time. Don't let your dream suffer because your emotions can't fall in line. This is your time to pursue them finally, don't look back and don't get discouraged.

Confidence is important for bringing your dream to pass. You must be confident when pursuing and presenting your dream to others. When you have a dream, everyone around you becomes investors. People will respect your dream when they see your level of confidence in it. If you go to present your dream to a group of people and you have little confidence, they will start to question if it's worth giving their attention.

Your confidence can be the determining factor whether your dream will be a success. Some people believe that what they have to offer is important. The crucial thing about confidence is that without it your dream is dead. If you don't have the confidence while you are presenting it to me, I won't have the confidence to invest in you. Even if you are unsure of whether your dream will be a benefit to others, your lack of confidence would be robbing them of the opportunity to sample your dream at its best. The reality is that we all need each other, so please be confident in your dream whether it's a business, or organization, I guarantee, it is bound to be the solution to someone else's problem. Stay enthusiastic and confident as much as you can.

## 3. Research and Planning

Research is an important part of bringing your dream to pass. Research ensures that you dot all your I's and cross all your T's. Most people really don't care enough to complete this step because it can be very time-consuming and depressing. Sometimes when you research, you find more obstacles than opportunities. When you approach this, it should always be done with prayer. I've seen people get to this step and get discouraged which eventually causes them to give up on a dream. The reason being is because research can tell you whether your dream is worth it, affordable and realistic. When you start to research, you must keep in mind that your dream is already worth it.

Nothing should be able to take you off your dream, not even research. If you believe in it, have the enthusiasm and confidence about it, then there should be nothing able to separate you from seeing your dream happen. Your budget is going to be your sponsor as you fulfill your dream. While on this journey, you must be strategic about your finances. Tell your money where it's going to go so that your dream can be as successful as possible. If you do not have a budget, you are limiting your ability to maximize your dream potential. Your dream is only as big as your finances will allow. Don't be afraid to reach out to people to sponsor you, what I've found is that people don't mind sponsoring for a dream or a project that they believe in.

The amazing thing about research and planning is that it serves as a bulletproof vest that protects your dream. The more you know about how to pursue, build, and protect your dream the stronger and more secure it becomes. Sometimes the reason that dreams fall through, or businesses fail is because there was a lack of research. Cost, budgeting, presentation and marketing are all areas that need to be thoroughly researched and planned out in order to ensure a bulletproof dream. Whatever you do, never discredit your research because that is what will tell you all the practical things you need to know about bringing your dream to pass.

### 4. School and Training

If your dream requires you to attend school or some sort of training, it is important that you consider the right one. If it is necessary to go to school, just know that when you come out you want to be ready to work and hit the ground running. Some of us dreamers really believe that we don't need to attend school or training, but what we fail to realize is that this is the most crucial part of fulfilling our dream. If you do not educate yourself first, you may find yourself in a terrible situation trying to make moves that you never knew existed and doing things that you were unprepared for. You cannot rely on your natural abilities or just your gifts alone. Your skills and abilities are natural gifts; gifts are abilities you were born with, or something developed through experience and training. Allow yourself a window of time to train and develop yourself for your dream. Whether we like to admit it or not, our dream will flow much smoother if we have the experience prior to jumping into the deep end. When you get the training and experience on top of your skills and natural gifts and abilities you are more equipped to complete your dream and it is less likely to fail.

## 5. Formatting and Presentation

Whether you are starting a product line, a stationary business or a ministry, the formatting and presentation is one of the most important steps for bringing your dream to pass. The way you organize and put things together is going to determine how well people receive your dream. There's no way you can have a million-dollar dream with a two-dollar package. This is not to say that you need to have a ton of money, but what you do spend on your dream must be well worth it. I am always someone who is big on quality; if something does not look good to me, I just won't buy it. It is true that a book is judged by its cover, so your dream needs to be wrapped with the best of the best. It needs to always hold the standard of a professional image.

When it comes to your dream you cannot afford to settle for less than what you first envisioned. For instance, rushing can make you lose sight of your original vision without understanding that it was the original vision that kept you excited in the first place. My point is you should view your dream like it's a product even if it's not; the packaging of your dream has to be equal to, or higher than your original vision. If you don't feel you have what it takes to complete the formatting of your dream, then you must connect with someone who is able to help you. While formatting and presentation can sometimes be a tricky thing to do, you must not lose sight that when it's all said and done, you will have a finished product and you will realize that it was all worth it.

### 6. Marketing and Networking

You must explore every possible marketing opportunity out there that will help you to fulfill your dream. This includes marketing materials, classes and seminars. Whatever steps are necessary to give you the proper marketing platform is what you need to explore. This is also a big deal when it comes to bringing your dreams to pass, because it requires diligence and discipline. The more people that know about your dream, the more people are likely to invest in your dream. The goal is to get as many people on board as possible, so don't be afraid to let people know about your dream. The amount of marketing that you do will always be the testimony to your efforts that bring this dream to pass. You must have a business mentality to see this happen. When I worked for an insurance company, they were big on marketing and networking. They stressed that no matter how many times you receive a 'no' it gets you closer and closer to your 'yes'. Remember you must market! Market! Market!

Marketing and networking may cost you time and money but is extremely necessary for you to pay now and eat later. Your marketing and networking are going to serve as the miles per hour for your dream. The speed or pace of your dream will be determined by the amount of consistent marketing you do.

Furthermore, people are interested in new dreams and ideas. You must keep in mind that somebody is waiting to hear about your dream, and you must not allow yourself to get into the mindset of excusing marketing and networking because you feel like your dream is unworthy. The wonderful thing about us is that without each other, we cannot go higher. We all need each other, and a smart business professional understands the power of marketing and networking. They understand that there may be someone out there who can perfect their dream which just might help the both of us. Keep in mind that there is always someone who has a piece of your puzzle, and the only way to find that is through network and marketing.

It's easy to feel like your dream is unimportant when you go to events, and you see people with easier solutions. You can slip into believing that your dream means nothing amongst other dreamers. Some dreams have a greater demand on them, but it doesn't mean that one is better than the other. If you have a dream of creating a custom Popsicle company in your city, but your companion has a dream of opening a children's hospital, you must not get discouraged in believing that your dream is stupid just because it doesn't look as impactful. Remember, your dream is the daughter of your purpose. That Popsicle Company might lead to a Popsicle factory and recreation center where kids can come and create as many custom popsicles as they desire. It may just so happen to sit right across the street from the hospital, which houses the children with cancer. This Popsicle factory may be the only place within walking distance for these kids to get away and enjoy themselves.

Never discredit the power of your dream. There is no such thing as a stupid dream, and there is no such thing as a more important dream. Whatever you do, do not be afraid to market and network, because remember, your level of confidence in your dream will determine the level of confidence that others have in your dream. Don't worry about how it appears to haters because if it was left up to them, you wouldn't have had a dream to begin with. True entrepreneurs would never discredit or look down upon another entrepreneur. Knowing how hard it is to get past your feelings long enough to achieve your dreams, you should have a level of compassion and respect for anyone else that is working hard to pursue their dream. Dreamer's respect other dreamers, especially when they know what it takes to bring a dream to pass.

Make sure your other steps are finished and you have a completed product or project before you begin to network and market. I was talking to my friend about her business that she wanted to start. She wanted to open a beauty supply store so I explained to her that she must be sure that she has a completed project before she starts to advertise and market. The reason being is because not everything will go as we plan, so the first time something comes up we will start to feel like we did not do a decent job on everything making the progress feel invalid, but that is not the case.

Someone can come in and say mean things such as "This hair is not quality hair; you need to shut this store down because it's a rip off." I told her that when this happens, she will not be discouraged because she will remember that she researched the quality of every piece that entered her store. Instead of feeling like she did not do a decent job at selecting her products, she will not be offended but instead, she will recognize that this customer does not know quality. For this reason, make sure that you complete all your steps before advertising, marketing, and networking because people are ready to criticize.

## 7. Discipline and Consistency

This is a step which sounds simple and easy to commit to, but this is one of the hardest things to do. Some of us have completed great projects, but because we lacked discipline and consistency, those projects were pushed aside. Many of us don't want to accept the fact that things don't happen for us because of our lack of consistency. Some investors will not support you just because you have a great product or business alone; they want to see your consistency, they want to see if you have stood the test of time, and they want to know how long you've been at this thing because your consistency shows them how serious you are. Perseverance is everything when it comes to completing any tasks whether it's school, work or starting your own business. Your determination, drive and commitment to your dream despite any opposition are all necessary for making it to the finish line.

Your dream must have most of your undivided attention so that you can ensure that it's completed to your expectation. To achieve this, you must stay focused because your dream depends on it. When you are working on your dream, you don't have much room to play around. If you feel your dream burning within you, there will be very few things that should be able to throw you off. Stick to the plan and let nothing take you off course. Some people will try to get you to abort your dream by sucking you in to their drama-filled lives which can make you emotional. While you are walking out, your dream you cannot let your emotions dictate your progress.

All sorts of things will try to distract you such as relationships, family issues, financial issues and more. Move past how you feel, and I'm telling you that when this happens you will feel like a conqueror, not just because you completed something, but because you had enough determination to move past your emotional self. A person who can conquer their own emotions is one who is unstoppable.

### 8. Set a Deadline

Every dream should have a suitable deadline. If your dream is important, you will most definitely set the most appropriate deadline for it. This deadline must not be too far that you have room to slack off, and it must not be too close to where it can discourage you if it doesn't happen. Take into consideration others who have completed the same dream, did your research and tried to find a reasonable deadline for it. Understand that your dream could be completed in phases, so there may be more than one deadline that needs to be set. A deadline gives you accountability to your dream and makes certain that you have little room for distraction.

Unbelievably, people are more receptive when you tell them that you can't hang out because you must meet a deadline, as opposed to telling them that you're working on a project. For some reason, people would rather be rejected with your deadline than your honest desire to want to reach your dreams. If they are truly your supporters, they will not make you compromise your dream. Instead, they will want you to not only work towards it but achieve your dreams on time. You must set a deadline and stick to it because your dream is most dependent upon you. Make it your priority to reject any form of guilt so that you can effectively work on your dream. When it's all over with, others will be proud of you, and you will be satisfied with yourself. Once you have achieved one dream, there is no turning back and you should have strong confidence that the other dreams are but a thought away from happening.

Every day we should be doing something to achieve our goals. When you set out on the journey to fulfill your dream, you must commit yourself to doing something that gets you one step closer to making that dream a reality. The truth of the matter is that so many things will demand your immediate attention and your dream will be the first thing pushed to the side. All of us have major responsibilities that require us to give our full undivided attention, and this is very understandable. For this reason, each day should be dedicated to completing something that helps you fulfill your dream.

It's funny how many of us can be more dedicated and committed to another person's dream, but when it comes to our own, we are relaxed and nonchalant about it. We see our dream as something we don't have to work on, as something that can wait. Some of us know we need to go back to school and complete our degree so we can land that dream job. For whatever reason, it is looked at like more of a task done in our leisure time such as a hobby rather than a required responsibility which is essential for our livelihood. I do not discriminate against people who are content with not doing anything to complete their dream. I am speaking to those who want it with passion, and desire clear direction on how to achieve it. My efforts in encouraging you are only to provoke the inner motivation that you possess for fulfilling your dream. I want to see as many people succeed in life as possible.

This land was placed here for us to enjoy ourselves and to have fun, but as we all know life is temporary, so why not fulfill our dream before it's all over? I want to help you achieve your dream this year. Second thing, I want to challenge you to start taking aggressive steps in fulfilling your dream so that you can be complete, knowing that you are fulfilling your purpose in life. Notice that the main person who benefits from these two things is you. If you start your journey to fulfilling these two things, you will begin to feel whole.

***Peace in Your Mind***

As you are fulfilling your dream make sure that you keep your stress levels, because every day is not going to be easy, but you will get through easier if you understand how to maintain a peaceful mind. Many people quit their dream even though things are going well, and life is good. One of the reasons why this happens is because of the inability to handle the stress that came with the dream that they had. Keep your focus and remain peaceful knowing that as you keep going things will work out.

**Big Brother advice**

I went home to Sandusky Ohio one weekend to visit my family, and I was speaking to my older brother. I was telling him about the book, and he started to give me some good advice. He told me to make sure that everything is in order before I expose my dream to the world. He was explaining to me that the current year would be the year in which the foundation is laid. He encouraged me to commit myself to making this the year of preparation, then the following year would most definitely be the year of exposure. He told me to get everything in order and get ready to fire one bullet after the next so that I can go forward with an unstoppable force.

I admired this advice from him because I can easily see that when everything is not completed prior to launching whether it is exposing our dream to the world, or starting a business, it can be more difficult and discouraging to finish. People want to know that you have a well thought out idea and if your plan is bulletproof. Until you get everything together, you give people nothing. Set your deadline and give nothing until you meet that deadline.

**Dream Accountability Partner**

Many of us have our dream mapped out and some of us have already exceeded these steps. An accountability partner is very much needed for anyone who is fulfilling their dream. When I first began drafting this book, I expressed it to a few people and everyone seemed incredibly happy for me, I had people who were holding me accountable. I will forever be grateful for my friends and their sacrifice and support of me completing this book. We would talk every day about business and how the book was coming along. It was so amazing to have others who viewed the light of my dream like I did. It was like every time I made progress, I had someone to share the news with.

Be sure to find an accountability partner who is just as excited as you are. The accountability partner that you choose must also have a dream that they are pursuing. The relationship is not healthy when it's one-sided because the accountability partner may feel used after a while. It's very important for you to support that person as well. If you are holding them accountable, and they are holding you accountable then no one can be selfish in believing that their dream is more important than the other. I suggest you only have one accountability partner, because if there is more than one, the attention could eventually go from the dreams that you all want to fulfill, to trying to balance the relationships.

If you're holding another person accountable for their dream along with yourself on top of the third party, it could possibly rob you of focusing more on your dream.

***The power of words***

Some of us have faith to try our dreams but no desire to speak over them. Our words carry power and authority, whatever you speak is exactly what you'll get. You have it within your power to make your dream as big as you want it to be. You also have it within your power to kill your dream from the root. When you speak positively in general, you position yourself to receive positive things.

Whatever words you decide to speak into the atmosphere will eventually come back to you in the same frequency in which you sent them. Don't be afraid to say what you want your dream to look like, if you believe it will happen just as you say.

It's very hard for me to surround myself with people who speak negatively about themselves or other people. When people start to say things like 'It will never happen for me and I'm not good enough, or that's just a fantasy,' those are the exact words that will come back to bite them. This is why our words should always be words of life. I challenge you to start speaking positive things about your dream, and you will not be disappointed as those positive words will begin to come back to you over time.

There were times when I would question if I was supposed to write. I kept having these negative thoughts that would tell me my words were not powerful enough and that no one really wants to hear what I have to say. All types of thoughts were flowing through my mind telling me that I am not educated enough to write a book, that my vocabulary is not extensive enough, and if I put my book out people would see how ignorant my thoughts were. Whenever I heard these thoughts, I would begin to speak the opposite. I would tell myself Heaven Brown is a woman of purpose; she is a woman of great creativity. No matter what people perceive me to be, Heaven Brown will always be known as a woman who pursued her dream. The unfortunate thing is most of us are too embarrassed to pursue our dreams. If I received an objection in my mind about my education, I would at once counteract that with a positive thought. Sometimes we blame other people for their negativity. The reality is we have the power to shut down and rebuke negativity even if it's coming from another person or even our very own thoughts.

My point is that we cannot discredit our dream or listen to negative thoughts or negative people because your dream has the power to change a life. As I began to go on the journey of fulfilling one of my desires, I started to feel a burning desire to share these things with the people around me. So, it is my hope that you will have a life-changing experience with this book. I pray that it will ignite a fire within you as you pursue your dreams. Whether you are an author or entrepreneur,

*Your Dream Your Responsibility*

someone is waiting for you and your dream. I want my dream to have so much influence that I'm blessed, and my children's children are also blessed. I always pray that my dreams go beyond my grave so that 50 and 60 years after I'm gone, my dreams can still influence the generations to come.

# Chapter 4
# Dream connection

**It's a connection issue.**

  So many of us genuinely want to go after our dreams in life and fulfill our purpose, but it seems harder and harder no matter how much effort and hours are put into it. Sometimes we think we are constantly making wrong turns and bad decisions. More than likely It's a connection issue, people sometimes make bad decisions because they are not properly connected to the right people. When you have the right connection, it's easy to get into the doors that open for you. Connection alone, depending on how you see it is a golden ticket into the doors that you wish to walk through. When you know the right people and you have the right connections, who can really stop you? Because you don't know the end from the beginning, it's hard making decisions that you are unsure of. Connection gives you a big advantage in life.

***Dream Connection***

Dream connections are those that are necessary for everyone to win. Have you ever met a person and you realized that they are connected to you because of the dream that they have, and you're connected to them because of the dream that you have? It's a wonderful thing when you have two people who are motivated about similar things as it's not every day you get to partner with like-minded people. You may have people who understand your dream and everything that you're telling them, and they may be genuinely happy for you, but it is not the same as having someone just as motivated as you are. The blind cannot lead the blind, and it is important for your circle to be filled with people who are heading in the same direction as you.

If you don't pay close attention to the people you allow within your inner circle as you're fulfilling your dream, you will get to a place where you will have to drop them off, especially when their plan is to head down a different route. When I was around 11 years old, I created a pattern with one friend who I was close to, she and I did everything together. It was so peaceful having that one friend simply because there was not a lot of chaos. Then, when the season was up for us, I gained another friend, and so did she. Neither one of us was angry at each other for going our separate ways as most 11-year-olds are. As I got older, I had many friendships that ended this way. As I reflect, I realize this is healthy.

We must learn to recognize when our season is up for the people in our lives. Letting someone overstay their season can mean bad business for the relationship and everything involved in it. Some of us have people in our lives that we know are no longer supposed to be there. Some of us allow people to linger around because we are bored or feel lonely without them. Some people can only be on your dream journey with you for a season, so don't be bitter about the relationships you had to leave. You may have needed to disconnect to get where you are especially if the relationship became stale. When you are on a journey, you must always be selective with your company. Your Dream depends on it.

There comes a time when we must evaluate the people who are connected to us to make sure that there is still juice flowing in the relationship. When things begin to dry out and get stale, this is when issues arise and tension increases. But stay connected to those who have your best interest at heart, and you have their best interest at heart. I'm talking about people who are connected to you because of the dreams you have, or the dreams they have that are fueling the relationship for the better.

### Does your dream match your personality?

When your personality matches your dream, you will notice that your dream will attract the right connections. Anyone who is pursuing their dream in life must consider whether it matches their personality. Your dream should be a direct reflection of your personality. Many of us like to pursue things because others have pursued them, but if it does not match your personality, and you are not passionate about it, it will not fit your lifestyle and you might not be successful at it. Under normal circumstances you will not find a boxing champion in a hair salon cutting and styling hair unless that's his passion. It just wouldn't fit his personality, especially if he's had no prior experience or desire to open a hair salon, other than the fact that his buddy did it and is making decent money. I'm not suggesting that you should not shoot for your true desires;

I am simply saying that there are parameters for personality types when it comes to fulfilling your dream. We have no business trying to do something because someone else has done it. Make sure your dream is your dream and not someone else's.

Often, we love to do things we do not have a passion for, this is why you see people who start business after business and none of them succeed. They were copycats rather than creators. Be sure to check and double check your desires prior to starting your dream. This is only so you can guarantee that this dream is yours and not just yours because someone else is doing it. You will know that the dream is sincerely your own if it has been tested by time. If you had a dream at one point and that desire never left, then I would say you're probably safe. If you've had a dream and the passion is still new after a year or two this is probably something, you want to take seriously enough to pursue.

When your dream starts to manifest and unfold, people will begin to give you feedback, they will start to say things like 'I always knew you would be a nurse' or 'that fits you'. If your dream fits your personality, you will always walk into it effortlessly. When you are doing something that you love and it fits your personality and desire it won't be stressful, but rather organic, fulfilling and exciting. Keeping true to the lane that you thrive in is key to fulfilling your purpose.

**Who can dream your dream for you?**

When I was 19, I went to a career Academy to get my (STNA) State Tested Nursing Assistant license. The reason I went for it was because as a little girl, I always loved to take care of my uncle, who had a stroke and was extremely sick. My grandmother noticed it right away; she began to tell me that I was a caregiver and that when I got older, I would take care of people. She told me I might even be a nurse one day.

All of this was wonderful news

because as a kid I thrived off what my grandmother saw in me. Her insight meant everything, so much so that I frame my purpose from her advice. The reason is because it gave me comfort to know that what I was doing was making her proud, so her positive affirmation and feedback always encouraged me to take the advice and run with it. As soon as I graduated high school, I began to take these classes, keep in mind my grandmother said I could do this. My mind told me that if my grandmother saw me as a caregiver from when I was a child, then I should have no problem getting this license and starting this career.

I went on to work in the MRDD community before I moved to a nursing home setting. I did this work over the course of four years. Towards the end of my career in this field, I was an activities assistant. I went throughout the nursing home helping the customers stay entertained. I would address their cognitive, social, and spiritual needs and sometimes their learning development. I realized that I was more effective as an Activities Assistant than I was as a nursing assistant. I liked to take care of people physically, but to do it for a living was not something I gained a lot of fun from. This is what informed me that it was never my passion to begin with.

At the new hire orientations, they explained how the nursing assistant positions should only be an option if the individual has a passion for it, and that anyone who is not passionate enough for the line of work is only likely to last a maximum of four years. It's obvious that they were right because by the end of those four years, I was burned out. I didn't want to look at another scrub uniform; neither did I want to drive past a nursing home, the whole idea of working in the nursing home as a nursing assistant made me feel like I was a prisoner.

The reason I shared this story is because even though this was never my dream it was a wonderful experience and pivotal for my path. I don't believe that this was my grandmother's dream for my life either; it was just a simple way of acknowledging my efforts and opening my eyes to the possibilities of becoming a phenomenal nurse someday. All parents and grandparents want their children to explore good careers and have a nice income someday. I genuinely believe that this was my grandmother's innocent way of encouraging me to put my skills to use someday.

Another point I am trying to make is that we should never do something because other people expect us to, as the only person who will suffer the consequence is you. Make sure that your dream matches you and is not someone else's dream for you. In my case it worked out for my good because this nursing path connected me to so many wonderful people. As we grow in life, we cannot discredit the seasons of our lives that prepared us for today. I thank God for my grandmother who encouraged me to follow my dreams. Even for the smallest achievements she was so proud of all her children and more than happy to experience life with us.

**Make a choice and go your way.**

When you are in the valley of decisions you will concern yourself with what door to choose. You cannot think too much about which one will be the right door. If you went through one door and terrible things began to happen at that job, such as having disagreements at work or being fired: you shouldn't regret it because you never knew what dangers were behind the other door. Don't focus on the negative things that are coming against you as a result of the door that you chose. Be ok with your decision and Listen to your heart; understand your views and your approach to your dream, so that you can go forward with an authentic, genuine heart for fulfilling it.

**Choose Wisely**

If you are dating or marriage and you are pursuing your dream, this chapter is important for you. If you talk to other people who have been through the same circumstance, they will probably tell you that your spouse can either bring life or death to your dream. Your relationship will influence your dream significantly for the good, or for the bad. My goal is to help you to understand that your partner in life is going to have an enormous impact on how successful you are and everything that you do.

Women in particular struggle with having a husband who she is willing to submit to, while men struggle with having a wife who is willing to help him strive towards his own vision. It seems that when two people have two completely different visions for their life, they sometimes they don't find out until after they are married, and things begin to spiral downward. Here you have a man with a great call on his life, but his wife has a different dream and no plans to share her husband with the world or vice versa.

If your spouse has a stationary job and you have a dream that you are pursuing for the benefit of the family that requires you to travel, understand that until you reach that level of sustainability there are sacrifices that everyone needs to be on board with. I see marriages fall apart all because somebody was not willing to make that simple sacrifice that would have positioned them for one of the best marriages that this world has ever known.

### *My public figure*

If your dream consists of you being in the public eye continually then you really need to be selective about the spouse that you choose. Often time's Celebrities are the most targeted in this area of their lives. They live in the public eye; their life is not a private matter at all. I'm sure politicians, entertainers, and celebrities can testify that people are more interested in the personal intimate details of their lives, than they are seeing them and their family happy.

Marriages don't often survive when they are constantly on display for everyone to view and criticize, and being a public figure makes it harder as you can't say "I don't want to be in the public eye any longer." It's not like a traditional job where you can call off or not show up whenever you please. Your wife can't say she doesn't feel like being around all the attention as it doesn't work like that. Even after a divorce or separation, you are going to forever be a point of interest.

If you are a public figure or aspire to be in the public eye, understand that people are always going to look through your window even if you close the blinds. You'll have no privacy or control over your life, and you are likely to be constantly abused and misunderstood. If you do not have a suitable mate by your side, it will be exceedingly difficult to be on your dream cloud and survive.

**The selection processes.**

When it comes to the dating life, I discriminate against a man by his relationship with God, the way he speaks to me and others, his energy, his looks, his age, his sense of humor as well as his education versus his experience. The reason that I am so meticulous is simply because I know what I want my future to look like, and I believe I'll know when I've found the right teammate to join me. Preparation is everything, and most marriages are too rushed, and the opportunity to carefully select the right person is given up because of lust, infatuation, or plain old eagerness.

Everyone chooses in their own way. I would rather wait and marry the right man then to suffer and marry a person that my life was never compatible with. This is one area of my life that I feel is important because when you have started to achieve your dream, it can literally be destroyed by marrying the wrong person.

# Chapter 5
# The Biggest Hindrance is Fear

**Fear and distraction**

Fear and distraction are probably the two main reasons why you haven't fulfilled your dream. These are common obstacles that can be overcome at any time. If you are someone who believes in your dream enough to overcome these obstacles, then you will get there. Both are direct and indirect devices used against you to get you as far away from your dream as possible. Fear encourages us to lose all faith, not only in ourselves, but in our dreams too. When we experience fear, we get distracted with various obstacles that are designed to completely throw us off course, so that we are unable to fulfill our purpose.

When you are fulfilling your dream, you will start to see distracting connections come your way to discourage you and get you off course. Problems will start to come about, causing your emotions to stir up to the point that you won't have any new ideas – Also you can get more responsibility such as work, family and other life issues to where your attention is no longer focused. Make sure you always stay on guard and are always aware. Some of them you would see coming, and others may take you by surprise. Nevertheless, stay the course.

### *Your Mind's Battlefield (fear)*

Every battle that you have will first begin in your mind before it manifests. Sometimes we believe that other people are our enemies when we are usually our own worst enemy. Here's how the battle begins. We must understand that the enemy's desire is to directly and indirectly steal our dreams. Directly, he tries to steal it with fear in our minds. Indirectly, he tries to purchase it with distractions. I am going to open your eyes to the trickery that is against your dream. Your dream holds so much value, which is why it should cost you everything. Your dream in its entirety represents a complete work, which carries the capacity to be a blessing to so many people.

If I were an enemy sent out to destroy you, the first thing I would come for is your dream. If I stop your dreams from happening, that gives me the opportunity to hinder the dreams of the people directly connected to you, such as your family and friends. Fear is something that is not usually brought up in everyday conversation. No one wants to admit that the real reason they are not pursuing their dream is because they're fearful in their minds. We always have a crutch and an excuse for why things are not working out. Most of us are afraid of failing and looking bad. Fear creeps in and says: "It will never happen for you; you know you can't do this; no one is on your side." The spirit of fear will make you feel as though nobody cares.

When you're a strong individual, sometimes you will be tested in areas that you don't know you are already equipped to pass. Before I authored this book I had so many doubts, it wasn't necessarily people whom I feared, but rather a fear of disappointing myself. Little did I know I had every resource I needed to complete the project before I even started.

Fear is common amongst most of us looking to pursue anything in life. Fear is an enemy embarking on the territory of our minds with a desire to steal, kill and destroy every good thing that exists. Fear creates a stronghold in our mind so that we cannot move forward in life. Fear is not always detected and usually goes under the radar because it is the norm and has been there so long. Some of us have business ideas and dreams of becoming someone great. We know the proper steps to achieving these goals for ourselves, but because of this fear we refuse to go forward. Some of us are more afraid of what people think or how they will look at us than we care about seeing our dreams happen.

For some reason today, people are afraid of others superseding them and being more successful in their endeavors. Subconsciously knowing this, we never want to be looked at like we're trying to outdo or be better than our peers. Your fear may also be that it's not the right time, or that you don't have all the resources that you need. You may even feel like you're too young. These things may be true but it's no excuse to fear going forward. All you need to do is position yourself and properly prepare, so that when the time comes you are ready for take-off. The 'little ole me' mentality must stop, because if it can happen for one it will happen for another.

### *People Pleasing Fear*

People pleasing fear is the most intense and mentally draining. It will have you saying things that you know others want to hear, because you're afraid that they will disagree with anything that comes from your mouth. This comes with a lot of distress as it feeds on your self-esteem. Usually with this fear, you're always trying to please other people so much that you are the one to suffer.

We must come to a place where we decide that we will no longer run from other people's belief in us. We must be courageous, and face that the only way through is to have an 'I don't care what you think' mentality. Some of us have made mistakes in our pasts that we are not proud of; maybe it has been a mistake toward someone very close to us. Even in our past mistakes we ought to have no shame. Living in fear and being tormented by what other people think is like slowly committing suicide within. You were not born to commit suicide. You were born to pursue your dreams and fulfill your purpose in life.

## *File Bankruptcy on Fear*

Fear will have you fortify yourself so that no one can find you and remind you of anything that happened in your past. Fear will cause you to isolate yourself because you don't want anyone to hurt you again. It will have you worried, confused and ashamed. The way I see it, worry is the best friend of fear. The effects of worry usually produce fear, neither are real, they are two enemies that come to make you believe that your life is over.

Fear has its effects on the human body, which can trigger stress levels to go up causing high blood pressure. Nerve damage is also caused through worrying too much. If this is you, can't you see that holding on to fear is costing you more than you can afford to pay? I know someone is reading this and saying, "But you don't know what I've been through, it's bad and I don't know how to recover." Well, my friend, I will tell you this, if it is that bad, then you need to file bankruptcy in that situation.

When I say file bankruptcy, I mean first accept how this situation has affected your life and if it has gotten so out of your control then there is probably not much you can do to change it. You'll never get anywhere by stressing over something that you can't help. However, you can let it go. Bankruptcy allows you to say, "Yes my situation has become so bad to the point that I need a new start, so I'm taking my life and I'm starting afresh, no more fear, no more shame, no more worry and no regrets." This declaration will empower you to walk in your purpose without guilt and shame following you everywhere you go.

### The Box Doesn't Fit

Most of the fear and shame that people experience usually has to do with their lack of confidence. Some of us are afraid to be ourselves because it costs us everything. There should never be a compromise, simply because all women, men, boys and girls have something unique and particular to offer to this world. If this was not the case, God would have surely made us all the same. We are all gifts wrapped in diverse ways with distinct colors, shapes and sizes.

One thing that I noticed about myself is that when I was younger, I dealt with a lot of insecurities, mainly because of other kids teasing me. Every child need someone to protect their emotions and because I didn't have this emotional protection growing up, I looked for it in other people, particularly men. Somehow, I knew I was unique and different, but I also thought I was weird and crazy. I was teased and called names that really hurt by my friends and peers, but because I wanted to be strong, I never allowed anyone to know how hurt I was. I knew I didn't fit into the box that people wanted for me, so I made a conscious decision to protect myself at all costs. The person that I became was a defensive, strong, independent, overbearing and protective woman. Without having a mother and a father in my life, I naturally jumped into those roles.

This was not always a good thing. I looked up one day and found that it was hard for me to be vulnerable to anyone. People thought I was very harsh and mean. I even had a woman refer to me as being too controlling. I believe the original design of a woman was to be vulnerable and strong without being overbearing and controlling. After reading a book called 'Captivating' by John and Staci Eldredge, I understood the true role of a woman. This book helped me to understand that it's okay to be as soft, loving and gentle as I want. I believe this book is for every female out there because it helps us to understand the true heart of a woman, and it includes things that we don't know about ourselves.

### Where is the Real Me?

During my childhood, I remember times when I showed people the real me; I revealed my true thoughts, attitude and personality. However, somewhere after I turned 20, I looked up and realized that I had lost touch with my true self. I was in a crisis because I had been missing for years. Now, I have become so unidentifiable, I don't know when I lost myself or even how to get back to being that person. I allowed people to crush my heart because I didn't know who or where the real Heaven was. When a person loses touch with who they are, they're usually at their most vulnerable state, because they often cling on to the first person that comes along and offers them a sense of belonging.

### There's Only One Me

For some reason I grew up thinking that the person that I am is not accepted in this world. Naturally, I took on the personalities of the people around me, not understanding that there is only one me that this world has to offer. No one told me that it was okay to be myself, so I hid behind goofiness to cover up the real me. I felt as if everything I liked or the way I would express myself was not commonly acceptable. The box that I lived in made me ashamed and uncomfortable whenever I would step out and be myself. I was always undecided about everything, feeling like I needed the opinions of others for approval. This thing called rejection, which victimizes people especially people of creativity, is something you cannot allow to hinder you. If you are one who is dealing with an identity crisis in this world, know that you are the only one who can be you. There's only one person who thinks exactly like you think, who talks exactly like you talk, and who can do exactly what you can do.

I think it's so sad when I see people trying to be like everyone else, it all boils down to one simple thing. Everyone is fearful of being themselves nowadays, for some reason, none of us like the person that we really are, let alone the unique creativity that we bring to the world. Understand that if you are going to follow your dreams, you must be okay with always being yourself, even if the environment suggests that you need to act like someone else. When we choose to take on another personality, not only are we stealing identities that don't belong to us, but we are also offending our maker. This behavior suggests that He made a mistake when He created you.

If we want to go forward in our dream with full confidence, we must be satisfied with the person we were created to be. You must be okay with your voice, your ideas and your personality. I don't see anything wrong with making minor changes to enhance these areas for the good, but to completely transform yourself into another person is to suggest that the original work was a mistake. Keep in mind that you respect yourself the most when you feel true to yourself and are walking in who you're created to be.

# Chapter 6
## Fear of Rejection

**Fear and Rejection**

In pursuing your dream, it's likely that you will develop a fear of people rejecting you, but it is so important that you don't allow this to get in your way. When I started to fulfill my dream, I had to step out from my comfort zone and connect with new people; this was so that I could let other business owners know who I was and what I had to offer. If I would have allowed the fear of getting rejected by those, I needed to connect with takeover; I would not have fulfilled the important steps toward my dreams. By becoming so fearful that it stops you from pursuing your dream, you are literally hindering a part of your purpose in life.

My friend and I were sitting out at a pool one day; her niece and another young girl were swimming at separate ends of the pool. Both little girls were around the age of 11. They were very anti-social and did not try to play with each other. We figured that they were distant because they were unfamiliar with one another. A few minutes later another young girl, 4-year-old Catlin came along and jumped in the pool with them. This little girl was so full of life and had a big personality; she started to play and socialize with both girls. When we looked up again, they were all laughing and playing tag together.

As we watched their interaction, we discovered that Caitlin's ability to get the other two girls to play together was because of her lack of fear. With them being older, they had already faced rejection and fear of acceptance to some w. When we are young, our innocent minds tell us that anyone can be a friend. We have no reservations in expressing our true feelings, but as we get older, we often lose that and experience hurt and rejection, which cause us to be more comfortable with keeping ourselves reserved. At some point, to move past the fear of not being accepted, we must acknowledge that rejection will come regardless, but it doesn't have to hinder our dreams.

**Small Man, Big World**

At some point we all have that small man big world mentality; we look at everything and everyone as though they are higher and more qualified than us. I want to encourage you to understand; if you have a dream, know that you are already good enough for it. As you go through and complete the progressive qualifications such as the training and certification needed to fulfill your specific dream, people will automatically qualify you as well. Although you should not discount the power of connection, you do not need anyone's acceptance or approval to start following your dream. Your dream is a part of your purpose, and no one has the authority to tell you that you are not good enough for it.

**How Do You Dress?**

The reality is that other people will always size you up. The first thing they take note of is usually your attire; the second thing they are curious about is the way you speak. These two things can tell them within the first two seconds of meeting you whether they are going to be interested in anything that concerns you. Whether you are on the job, on an assignment or just randomly walking through a grocery store, people are watching. People watch other people; this is how we grow and develop as human beings.

If you're going to be professional, you can create your own style of professionalism that is acceptable for whatever type of dream or work you are pursuing. Whatever you wear, ensure that you are confident and content with it. Keep in mind, your opinion of yourself is what really matters. When you feel confident in the way you present yourself, you will be confident in your work, even as you're speaking to others. People usually know a confident person when they see one. Even though the world wants copycats, you can uniquely tailor your image to your liking. All I'm suggesting is that you should be yourself even in a world that tells you otherwise.

 I remember talking to a friend one day, and I asked her if she liked the shoes I was wearing. She replied by asking me if I liked them, I said "Yes," her next response was: "If you like them, why are you asking me?" Instead of taking offense to this, I got excited because she helped me to understand that I really shouldn't care about her opinion, or anyone else's for that matter. The truth is when you seek acceptance and approval from others; you will see that people all have different standards.

 On another occasion, I was

speaking with a few of my friends about my hair and how I should wear it. One of them said she likes it when it is long and curly, another friend expressed that she likes the short, angled bob look on me. Getting both opinions really confused me, simply because I enjoy both looks when they fit certain occasions. Please! Do not live your life trying to be accepted by others. If you do, you will always question yourself according to your assumptive thoughts of other people's beliefs of you, and this may make you feel rejected. Even when you know people are sizing you up, pay no attention to it; remain confident.

### How do We Speak?

Some of us are disqualified in our endeavors because of the way we speak. I know for me personally; I've always been very nervous about how my speech is received by others. I've had people tell me that I have a very soft girly voice and I've also had others say that I come across harsh. Sometimes when we go to speak to people, we are worried that we sound uneducated, too country, or maybe too urban.

All these things are a part of the battle within our minds. This battle is associated with fear, it can be easily annihilated if it is ignored and substituted for faith. On the other hand, if you are one who wants to tune up to your speech so that people can receive you in the way that you want, then you should position yourself. I believe you will gain confidence, especially when you know you have received corrections for proper speaking. Your interview skills will be sharper, and your approach to people will be acceptable to you, which will make them confident in you.

### *Pressure*

Many of us have serious pressure on our hands, which can lead to the fear of being accepted. Pressure as an adult is usually on another level of seriousness, this is because of the realistic moves that need to be made. Pressure begins in the mind of the victim. As a result of fear, we submit our actions according to what we believe the people around us will accept from us. There is no right or wrong way of being you and doing things according to the way you choose to do them.

It is true that pressure is real; people are constantly being judgmental about things that really don't matter. We need to get it in our minds that pressure is one of the main triggers for fear in both children and adults. Sometimes, we even accept peer pressure from those who have not actually pressured us about anything. Our assumptive mind tells us that this person is a certain way, and they will not respect our decisions. We jump to conclusions; if we think we know a person's character, we can automatically predict their views of us. Whatever you do, don't let your assumptive mind talk you out of your dream. More importantly do not let the pressure of outside opinions dictate how you make your moves towards fulfilling your dreams.

### *Executive Decision Maker*

When you are fulfilling your dream, you cannot allow too many people to give an opinion about the things that you are doing. When you extend the opportunity for others to give their opinion, somewhere along the line you may lose your original vision along with your own opinion. I believe, when it comes to the decisions that need to be made about certain things regarding your dream, you ought to be the executive decision maker. Reason being, when you start to let other opinions into the picture, your view can become clouded, and you become robbed of your authority on the matter. If this happens, it could be ridiculously hard to come back and regain control of your original ideas after that point.

Some people will try to give you their opinion just because they want a say in the outcome. They want to be able to tell people they did it for you, and you would not have completed it without them. Someone might want to help just so they can take the credit for your dream. Just be wise when you are getting any type of help or opinion from anyone else. It's sad, but there are people that will go so far as to say they made you; even though they know they did nothing for you. It's unfortunate but this will happen, and you must be very careful not to lose your executive authority over your dream. Remember that you are the sole founder and CEO of your dream; no one can take that from you.

***Fear of Families Opinions***

Many of us have family members we love with all our hearts. Naturally, the opinions of your family will mean everything to you. If you have a bad reputation with your family, this can cause you to be scarred and distant toward people. In this broken state, it is hard to fulfill your dream because the people who are supposed to believe in you are the main ones trying to tear you down. When you've made a mistake or you've lived a life that you regret, your family will be the first to remember and throw it in your face. This is discouraging altogether; you must understand how to handle the fear of your family's opinion before you can truly step into your purpose. For those who have families who are more supportive than negative, you are blessed and continue to keep that dynamic growing.

# Chapter 7
# Fear of failure.

**No More Hiding**

Naturally when we are afraid or fearful of rejection, we close ourselves up to the people that love us the most, and we live our lives in secret. This feeling of shame and rejection makes no real sense to our minds; the most logical idea is to hide. If you are one who is in hiding because of your past, and unable to start your dreams; I encourage you to tell the truth and be honest with yourself. If you are not first honest with yourself, you can't be honest with others, and you will walk around feeling shame and regret having your outside dressed to impress and you're inside empty. For this reason, my desire is not to impress anyone but to live in freedom and liberty. When shame and the fear of rejection no longer intimidate you, you are free to share your story and pursue your dreams how you wish.

### **Failure**

Failure is a word that can feel like a threat to people with fear. Failure is something that we all face when we are pursuing our dreams, there definitely will be times during the process that you feel like you failed. To feel failure, there must first be some sort of goal or intended aim that you set your mind to complete. The fear of failure is to entertain an intense anxiety in pursuit of a goal or mission that you feel might not be successful. Though the fear of failure is common, don't allow fear to be the conductor of your life.

### **What Others Think Shouldn't Matter**

Was there ever a time when you

noticed something awesome about yourself, but you wouldn't believe it until somebody gave you a shout out or showed you recognition? This is why some people will do nothing unless other people approve of it. The success of your dream should not be decided by the people who approve or disapprove of you.

Somehow you know that you are walking in your calling and your purpose, but it doesn't hit you until you see your face on TV, in a magazine or on the cover of a book. If we are not careful, validation from others can be the determining factor of whether we fulfill our purpose. What other people think of you should not be your concern.

### *A Dreamer's Imagination*

Dreams first began in our imagination. When we surround ourselves around people who have no dreams, it causes us to stop dreaming altogether. Most of the time, when people fear failing, they will often choose to not continue with their plans. Some people have dreams that they wish to pursue, but because of their fear of failing mixed with their fear of what others will think of them, they let their dreams die.

At first, all you saw was the dream, the finish line and the trophy, but the minute you became fearful, you thought of everything that could go wrong. You said to yourself maybe this is not a good idea, it might be too risky, I could break a leg, my rent is coming up maybe I should just wait. In the beginning, your focus was the big picture, you saw it and were determined that you were going to get it because your commitment to it was serious, but then suddenly you saw the bad picture and you started to freak out, you took a step back and wondered if it was ever supposed to come to pass in the first place.

Not everyone cares about your dream, but if you give your focus and dedication to your dreams, eventually people will join you on your cloud. Some of us have people around us who are very afraid of our dreams, but this is no reason to fear.

I believe a dream is a deposit from heaven into the bank account of your mind, which gives you the ability and the insight to make it visible here on earth. Some of us have people in our lives that we love who happen to be extremely negative and jealous hearted. Some of these people are brothers, sisters, aunts, uncles, cousins, spouses and even parents. Sometimes when we esteem people with high regard and respect, we take their views and opinions as our own. Therefore, if someone doesn't agree with your dream, it is easier to immediately fall victim to the fear of failure. Whatever you do, you should always allow your mind the freedom to rise above the fear of shame and failure.

Soon enough you will start to see your dream life in full effect. When these things start happening, you should have a tingle in your stomach that says, 'I'm not ready'. This sensation can be interpreted by your mind as a joyous fear; it will make you feel excited and nervous all at the same time. For some of us, we get sweaty armpits, sweaty hands and stuttering of our words. When this happens it's your body's way of telling you the moment you've been waiting for has now arrived, your dream is about to begin., brace yourself and get ready for what's about to happen next. This really is a beautiful place to be; even if you feel fear, it's a good thing. Just remember that the only person you want to strive to impress is yourself. Do not allow your mind to work against you or to tell you anything contrary to the truth.

*Your Dream Your Responsibility*

# Chapter 8
# Your Dream Will Declare War

**War**

When people have a dream, what they are really saying is that they would like to declare war. If you have a dream, it means that you are going to go against your current mediocre lifestyle along with various other opposing forces. Moving forward in your dream is almost the same as stepping on the battlefield. Before you pursue it, your mind must be prepared for battle in its entirety, whatever that may be. Your battle may be removing people from your life who could literally annihilate your dream. Your battle may even be a faith battle, where you have no choice but to stand on everything that you believe to be true so that you can fulfill your dream and ultimately achieve your purpose.

***The Vision Belongs to you.***

Don't let other people dictate your dream. You know the dream that is inside of you, you know what it looks like, what it sounds like and even how it feels. You're the only person who has a visual of what your dream is supposed to look like. Every part of your dream represents a desire on the inside of your heart, and eventually you'll start to understand more about yourself as you pursue it. It is hurtful when I decide to share my dream with someone and suddenly, they start speaking negatively.

Don't expect someone to see a vision that's invisible to everyone else except for you? Please save yourself from discouragement and don't mention it until the time is right. There's always someone waiting to tear down your dream cloud so that you cannot be on display. Some people genuinely believe they are giving you the right advice by secretly hinting that it's not a good idea. This is a sign that you should always be at war protecting your dream. These are the kind of people that I never mention my dream to, at least not until it's finished.

For some reason, humans love to give unwanted opinions in places that they feel necessary. Because of that reason, I'm strongly encouraging you to not share your dream with everyone. By no means am I telling you to run from rebuke, this is because sometimes rebuke can be a good thing. It can be the very thing that protects you during the process of fulfilling your dream. It is particularly important for us to have someone who holds us accountable for our dream and who is also extremely excited about it. Maybe this person is a mentor, friend or family member. Be sure that this person has no personal vendetta against you as not everyone has your best interest at heart.

Make sure that there is someone there to keep you focused and to provide encouragement, someone who wants to see your dream happen just as much as you do. Don't get discouraged by what people will say to you or about you. People talking about you should never be your motivating factor for fulfilling your dream, because at that point you're no longer doing it for you, but for the naysayers. Keep in mind that your dream will bless the right people and the right people will start to come and support and uplift you as you fulfill your dreams.

On your journey to fulfilling your dream, you cannot allow your circle to be filled with people who are intimidated by it. I've had people who I thought were for me and excited about the things that were going on, but all the while they were secretly praying against me. This is why you must not forget that when you begin to dream aloud, what you are really saying to the opposing forces is that you want war. Though opposition is normal you must always have a battle plan for your success.

If you know someone who you feel is pretending to care about you and your dream, then you may need to consider cutting that person out of your inner circle. As you go along and fulfill your dream, you will start to see those people who are truly for you. You will start to see people come your way, who you have dream connections with.

## *Relationship Distractions*

Some of us let distractions come into the picture, distractions that have nothing to do with our dream. Relationship distractions, for example, are the best ammunition for destroying a dream. If you are not careful, you will not understand that your relationship and your marriage can be the very thing that keeps you on course or takes you completely off course and will make it difficult for you to rebuild again. Some of us get connected with people who really don't care about us let alone our dreams. They want to use you for their own pleasure and benefit when it's convenient for them. So, when you talk to them about your dream it's almost like you're blowing dust in the air, it means nothing. The reality is that some people just can't be excited for you because they don't care about you. Being naive and thinking everyone wants the best for you is a lie and a trap they you cannot fall into.

I was in a relationship with a man who I thought would help me fulfill my dreams. I later realized that he had an ulterior motive. Had I known that I would get so hurt in that relationship beforehand, I wouldn't have allowed myself to get distracted in the first place. When it was all over, I realized that he did not care about me, therefore, my dream and my purpose meant nothing to him. When we make decisions using wisdom it can save us a handful of heartache.

Sometimes it's the people that are right underneath your nose. The ones you sleep with at night, that you think would want the best for you, but they want nothing for you. This type of discouragement coming from your spouse may not be intentional. You may feel that this person does not believe in your dreams because they're not as supportive as you would like them to be. In some cases, it may not be that the person is not supportive on purpose; it may have everything to do with the fact that they genuinely do not know how to celebrate others.

I used to know someone who did not know how to celebrate other people. She didn't know how to use positive words of affirmation like: 'I'm happy for you or that's good or how wonderful'. I couldn't understand what her problem was, but then one day it hit me, and I realized that she truly did not know how to rejoice with those who rejoice. If it wasn't her good news, she didn't know how to celebrate with me for my good news. This type of person is what you call a frenemy, they're not quite for you but they are not totally against you. Maybe you've never had any sort of run-in with them but at the same time they appear to be very nonchalant about anything that concerns you.

Spousal Support is important, when you have an unsupportive spouse, you cannot give them too much of your dream because when you start to tell them about it, their responses may be so bland that you will begin to question how valuable your dream really is. Even though they mean no harm it is in your best interests to spare as many details as possible. If you are in a relationship with a person like this and you're not sure of what to do, you must keep in mind that your dream was given to you, not them. You cannot be disappointed about anyone's lack of support, remember your dream is your responsibility.

Understand that every ounce of negativity that you permit in your life, as you're fulfilling your dream is going to feel equivalent to trying to grow a beautiful tree when someone keeps trying to chop it down. You may have a spouse who is not the least bit interested and is in fact against your dream, but you cannot let that stop you, because remember your dream is a link to your purpose.

My job is not to motivate you to believe that your dream will come without a battle or a struggle. Naturally, we all want things to be easy and we get very frustrated when they're not. You must have faith that when you set your heart out to complete your dream, it will happen to you. No matter what forces come up against you to make you fearful or to distract you it will happen if you believe it.

### *Distractions and Opposition*

Keep in mind that when you set out to fulfill your dream you must always be prepared for war. Distraction is a missile fired at us, which has a massive impact on the timing of our breakthrough and blessings. When we know that we are being distracted we genuinely need to exercise our self-will over these situations. The wonderful thing about distraction and opposition is that they are usually temporary. You might be distracted with one thing today, and when you overcome that thing, tomorrow you might be distracted with something else.

Though it is a powerful hindrance, all distractions have an end date. It's a beautiful thing to see someone wake up from their distraction. It's like one day they are distracted, and you wouldn't think they would snap out of it, but the next day they come to their senses, and they say to themselves "What was I thinking? I need to get back on track today!" When this happens, life says "Oh my! She's waking up, hurry up and find something else to distract her with." Though it's not usually something we discuss, the truth is life is a wonderland of distractions.

Let's say you were supposed to meet with someone one day but got distracted along the way. That distraction caused you to be late and miss your appointment. Unfortunately, this has happened to all of us at some point in our lives. Some of us battle distraction more than we fear. So again, the good thing about distraction is that it is only temporary and comes with an end date. The dreadful thing about distraction is that it can cause a delay in your finances, your business, your relationships, your goals, and ultimately your dreams.

Another disadvantage to distraction is the amount of enthusiasm is stolen from us. Have you ever had a dream or a desire to do something and because you were distracted along the way you lost your zeal? By the time you make it to your dream or goal you are too drained to give it your complete effort. You might even feel like you're too old to even pursue your dream again. These are the things that distraction inflicts on us.

Some things you may still want to do, but by the time you come around to it, there's no more energy. You had all the energy you needed yesterday to complete this task but not today because you allowed yourself to be distracted.

**Pursuing the Dream with No Energy or Zeal**

Distraction and laziness also come with a language; you can usually detect your level of distraction by the number of excuses you make. When you start making excuses for why you can't complete the tasks or dreams that you set for yourself, this is a result of distraction and laziness. 'I wish I could, maybe tomorrow, now is not the right time, who's going to help me? I'm just not ready, I'm just not strong enough right now, I don't have the money, and one day I will get to it.' These are the words of a person who is currently distracted and lazy. Usually, people who are distracted put their dreams on hold and they say, 'for now I will leave this.' Distraction is designed to keep you off-course long enough for you to lose your zeal. Your zeal means everything to your dream. It is the gas that fuels you even when it looks like it's impossible. Distraction will cause you to approach the dream without excitement. Some people had dreams from years ago that they were passionate about, so enthusiastic that when they talked about their dream, you could see the twinkle in their eyes.

Now the opportunity of their dream happening has stumbled upon them and because it has been so long, the fire for that dream has dwindled. It's like an NFL player who is about to play in the championship, he goes to the field, he has the uniform, he even has the fans on his side, but he has no real energy. He was all hyped up for the game, but his energy was stolen before he got there. This is what pursuing your dream with no zeal or enthusiasm looks like. This is why you cannot allow yourself to become too distracted or lazy.

**Opposition Brings Elevation**

You must understand that if someone is coming against your dreams, all it means is that they are pushing you to fulfill them. The opposition is not coming to destroy you, but it is coming to elevate you to your next level. Whatever you do, do not be afraid of the persecution that will arise because of you running after your dream, because without the small battles, you will not know how to persevere. Though your dream declares war on your mediocre life, you should look *at* your dream as your baby that you are sent to protect. No parent will allow anybody to hurt or harm their child. It is up to you to guard and protect your dream with your life. No one is going to do it for you; it is your responsibility to be the overseer of your own dream.

The way I see it, if you protect your dreams, eventually your dreams will reward you. They will be a testimony of your efforts that went forth to bring them into fruition. I encourage you to not let anyone wipe your dreams off the map. You have the key to your dream door, and you've been given the responsibility of making sure no one breaks in to steal or to destroy it. Remember, when you face challenges, they are only signs that there is more for you. Whatever you do, do not give into the 'woe is me' mentality, you're required to win any war that rages against you're dream. You must never forget that you can overcome every obstacle-be it distraction or any form of opposition because you are already equipped with the necessary weapons to conquer.

## Chapter 9
## *While living your dream life*

This is the place where your dreams have truly happened. No longer are you working to accomplish your dream, but you are working to maintain it. This is where it gets a little bit easier because the hard part was getting yourself and others to genuinely believe in it. At this point, you are officially positioned on your dream cloud. You have silenced every naysayer and hater, and no-one can deny that you are living in your dream. You've overcome the biggest objection which was you. This is a place where you are like a train on the move, and you are going too fast to stop. People are now expecting to see you on your dream cloud. It is at this place that your dream is attached to you, and it has manifested, so this is how they know you. When people talk to you, they have no choice but to ask you about your dream.

I am a very introverted person and I like to be alone more than I like to be around other people, so I see it as a good thing to have as few people around you as possible. When you are living your dream life sometimes people think that you are taking on recruits, so they try all types of manipulation just to get you to let them on your dream team. Some will try to make you feel bad by saying 'Don't forget where you come from.' If you are one who is currently living your dream life, I want to encourage you to not feel guilty or get discouraged and enjoy your dream life the way you want to and learn how to manage the challenges of your success.

When you are living your dream

life you will usually be busy, and sometimes you may not be able to hang out or talk on the phone like you used to. This is the place where your friendships will be challenged. When you were not living your dream, no-one got offended when you didn't call or text, but now everyone's offended. When you come to this place, you must remain humble, because people are going to throw as many darts at you as they possibly can. You might notice people being intentionally spiteful.

When this starts to happen, it can turn you into a bitter person and start to get to your head. In other words, if you're not careful you can slip into pride and think that you have arrived because of the haters piling up on you. Some people view haters as motivation, and instead of getting discouraged they start to enjoy the attention. There must be a balance if you want to genuinely enjoy yourself on your dream cloud. You must not allow people to tear you down, and you must be careful so that other people's opinions cannot make you see yourself more or less than what you are. You should also not allow the opinions or actions of how people feel affect how you move.

**_Not everyone belongs in your circle._**

When you are living the dream, not everyone should be allowed in your life. Truth is, just like you had people who criticized you for achieving your dreams; you will most definitely have people that will try to tell you how you should live your dream life.

Usually, the people who are in your life have direct access to you or indirect access to you. Just because they are part of your dream team does not mean they should be too close to you. Let's just say you have a T-shirt company. On your dream team, you may have a graphic designer who specifically does your graphics. You don't talk to him daily, but you acknowledge him in various ways because he does a good job of your graphics. You are helping his dream and he is helping yours. He is on the business end of your dream team. You also have others on your dream team like those who are in your life on a regular basis, such as friends and family. These are the people who are not offering you anything material for your dream, but they do offer support. They are most beneficial when they are close to you. The graphic designer is most beneficial for you from a distance.

### *Designated roles*

Everyone on your team needs to have a definite role and if those roles are not defined, we need to know when to step in and to define them. If you have set it up for one person to be the cashier as you are selling your jewelry at your jewelry parties, it means that the cashier cannot be a food server as their role is to specifically be the cashier. Everyone on your dream team needs to understand their role and they have also been okay with them.

### *Time of testing*

Some of us may experience some financial challenges that discourage us when it comes to fulfilling our dream. I believe that there are seasons where our faith is tested to see if we will give up or still believe. But in these testing's, you'll find that the testing is only to reveal what's on the inside of you.

When we go to school, we have exams that are usually set up to test everything that we've learned. The test is not there to embarrass you or make you look bad, but rather to praise you for all your hard work. At the end of every test, you will receive a reward according to your performance. The thing about a test is that no-one can do it for you, and no-one should be helping you. The test is to shine light on your strengths and abilities. Getting discouraged because you are in a testing season is ok, just keep in mind the test is to mentally condition you and is ultimately for your benefit. Understand that you will not test in an area that you were not already taught. If you are feeling tested, please understand that you have already been equipped for it. We need testing in our lives to help us constantly grow and endure challenges.

I recall going through a time of testing with a company that I worked for. It was a stressful and discouraging situation, I absolutely dreaded going to work every day and I remember often going out to my car to pray. This work situation was far from the vision that I saw for myself, and I knew that this was not what I imagined for myself. I wanted to give up and quit so that I wouldn't have to bother myself with the job anymore. I eventually finished my assignment at that place. They eventually let me go and finally the torture was over. If felt so good to finally be free from that employer. After this, I was financially able to not work a traditional job for eight months. It was during the eight months I began to get business ideas, speaking engagements. Sixty of those days were spent drafting this book.

When I look back at the testing, I realize that my character was on display before my very eyes and for people to see. I learned that the testing was set up for the impressive blessing thereafter. If I had quit, the cards would have played out a little differently. During that time, I received a big check that held me for my expenses until I completed everything that I was supposed to.

My desire is to not work for man, I realize that I am determined to have multiple streams of income that do not require me to punch a clock for someone else. My desire is to provide opportunities for others to fulfill their dream. So that time of testing brought out things that were in me that I never even knew existed. Sometimes this is what's required for elevation. A storm will come to help secure us in our next level. When you get promoted in a position, it's usually because you have proved yourself worthy for the title. I'm here to tell you not to get discouraged in your season of testing as it just means that you will be rewarded for your diligence. If you can endure the trials and tests coming against you right now, I guarantee you'll see what's on the other side of that storm, and how the trials and tests may have been for your own good.

**Burning Bridges on your dream cloud**

As human beings, we are naturally confrontational in some way. Even if you are not a confrontational person there's always someone who can press your buttons. It's very easy for a business deal to go sour even without that being your intention. When you are pursuing your dream, you will experience your share of jealous people. For this reason, you must not give in to any drama that will conflict with business or your dreams.

**Give back.**

When you are on your dream cloud it is especially important that you keep a mind of humility. We should constantly find ways to give back to people. Your dream cloud is the place where you have achieved your goal and things are looking well. This is the place where you cannot forget about the people who helped you get there along with the community of upcoming dreamers. You should not want to give back just so you can look good in front of people, it must be a genuine desire to see other people achieve their dreams as well.

This is especially important because your giving back should not have a selfish motive behind it, neither to be seen or for exposure, but from the depth of your heart. People need to know that you still care about others, and that it doesn't change just because you are on your dream cloud. Pursuing one dream is just the beginning of fulfilling your purpose.

Start listening to yourself; you will be surprised that many of the deep answers you seek are already right there inside of you. Take your dream journey seriously; it will have an enormous impact on your life. Your dream journey will unravel the dreams that have been in you. Do not be afraid to challenge yourself and do some soul searching, these are the keys that can take you to your next level, but you must first figure out what has been a hindrance. I'm excited about your new journey and most importantly your dream journey. God bless you.

*Your Dream Your Responsibility*

## *Farewell*

Thank you so much for reading this book. My hope is that you were encouraged and motivated to pursue your dreams. If you have already started, I pray that this book helped put things into perspective for you to take it to another level. I approached this book from a different angle than most. My heart kept telling me to be sure to mention the hindrances so that people can be aware of them. Most of us have things that have hindered us for years such as fear, distractions, social media, negative connections and even jealousy. We are often unable to get to the root issue, so my intention was to expose the hindrances so that the dreamer can move forward freely. I was always told that you cannot move forward with your future until you first deal with your past. Please do not cheat yourself; I encourage you to take that journey of searching out why your dream hasn't happened yet. If this book has truly inspired you to pursue your dream, then don't hesitate to tell me about it. You can connect with me by visiting my website at www.heavensspeaking.com I want to hear from you as soon as possible.

Heaven Brown

## *Acknowledgment*

I thank God first for giving me a second chance at life. There was a time when I didn't want to go on, a time when I didn't see a future for myself, but He showed me a light that I could not resist. His love and compassion towards me have given me the confidence to walk in grace, having no fear of the opinions of others. I also want to acknowledge my mother Evett for continually reflecting love. I also want to acknowledge my loving husband Ty for his support. I want to thank both my grandmother Ann, and my aunt Mae for raising me to be a woman of integrity. A special thanks to Mr. Larry and Mrs. Lola, who accepted me as an addition to their family when I was only 19. I want to acknowledge my cousin Aquarius who was one person that I sought wisdom from.

I want to thank my brother Kyree, Sister LaTasha and brother Laquan, for sharing wisdom and advice. I want to thank my sister Domilola. I appreciated her help with multiple revisions. When my spirit was down, and times felt rough, I would lean on my best friend Lisa for encouragement and positive words. A special thanks to my aunt Anekia for being my backbone. I also appreciate my friend Stacy for her support and dedication to this project with me. I want to give an honorable thanks to Drs. David and Tracy Forbes for grooming me to be on fire for the Lord and laying the foundation for my walk with God. And may God bless everyone who believed in this dream; I pray that this message is a blessing to you like it was to me. And remember your first audience is yourself.

# Heaven Brown

Made in the USA
Columbia, SC
22 May 2023